Rooftops
A Collection of Haiku

by

Xanthos Likes

About This Book

Written by: Xanthos Likes
Art by: Zerin Likes & Lily Goa
Cover Design: Lily Gao

Likes Publishing
Lilburn, GA 30047
Visit us at likespublishing.com

First Edition: September 2025
Library of Congress Cataloging-in-Publication Data

Names: Likes, Xanthos, author | Likes, Zerin, artist |
Gao, Lily, artist.
Title: Rooftops: A Collection of Haiku
Description: First edition. | Lilburn, GA : Likes Publishing, 2025. |
Summary: A collection of haiku with accompanying artwork.
Identifiers: LCCN: 2025914166 | ISBN 9798889021179 (hardcover)
| ISBN 9798889021186 (paperback) | ISBN 9798889021193 (ebook)
Subjects: LCSH: Haiku. BISAC: POETRY / Haiku.
Classification: LCC PS593.H3 L55 2025

ISBNs: 979-8-88902-117-9 (hardcover)
979-8-88902-118-6 (paperback)
979-8-88902-119-3 (ebook)
Printed in USA

ACKNOWLEDGMENTS

To a past, present, and future me: You will make it. It's just a moment.

To all people who are struggling to make it through: I hope you find a moment of peace, a moment of laughter, a moment of joy, or all three. Keep going, it's not over, things will get better.

Xanthos

Spends hours helping

Checking to make sure you're fine

And calls himself friend

Table of Contents

Rooftops 1

Mazes 3

Life 5

why 7

New year 9

potato 11

Mental Block 13

Deserts 15

Cars 17

Tea 19

Journeys 21

Expectations 23

Discord 25

Anxiety 27

Unrequited 29

Lonely 31

Escape 33

Flowers 35

Dejected poetry 37

Explanation/Apology 39

Ouch 41

Birthday 43

Escapist Dreams 45

Bees 47

Anxiety 49

Depression 51

Sugar 53

poetry 55

The trouble of haiku 57

Grandma 59

Family reunion 61

ASDF 63

Stabbing people 65

Sick day 67

Mark B. 69

Cheese 71

Sharing 73

human 75

Missing Reflection 77

Coward's conversation...................... 79

Discordant Self 81

time 83

Splat 85

Fears 87

Constellations................................ 89

Silly Reasoning............................... 91

Early morning haiku 93

Angst 95

Insecurity 97

Perspective 99

Impostor.. 101

Drowning...................................... 103

Everything's fine 105

Socializing 107

Dreams 109

what if-.. 111

learning.. 113

Hahaha haha ha............................ 115

Attention deficit............................ 117

words.. 119

My Friends 121

Unbounding.................................. 123

sharing words................................ 125

Antecedent Duplication................ 127

Motivation 129

Simple comfort.............................. 131

commonly unique.......................... 133

unabashedly unoriginal.................. 135

Craftsmanship 137

In touch 139

Goner.. 141

Anyone out there 143

Writing these 145

Scheming minds............................ 147

Friends pt 2.................................... 149

Knock knock 151
Jaded 153
Cowardice 155
Specialized Shyness 157
Burning out 159
Hi 161
Uninstall 163
Otherwise 165
Friday 167
Surrender 169
Missing 171
Simply Exasperated 173
Bad advice 175
Hidden costs 177
Out of stock 179
a Smile 181
One of those mornings 183
Busy 185
Whatever this is 187
Departing words 189

Rooftops

My last, greatest step

That will take me far away

And break my mom's heart

Mazes

I oft get astray

In a maze with no exits

But it's my own mind

Life

Finding a purpose

that keeps us from disaster

it's ephemeral

why

oh my why is hurt

is so much pain what the heck

please brain don't be mean

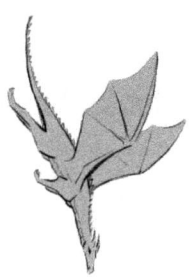

New year

Once again around

Same relative point in space

only to the sun

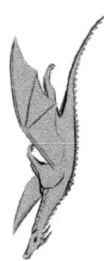

potato

buried in the ground

no need to deal with people

ideal conditions

Mental Block

So many thoughts fly

Trying to make their way out

Sealed inside my mind

Deserts

They say it's barren

Empty graveyards at life's edge

But life found a way

Cars

It's really boring

Sitting, waiting to arrive

But I'm not alone

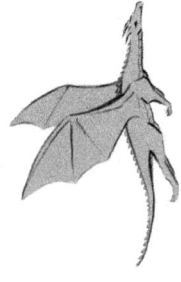

Tea

Everyone has things

They keep buried oh so deep

Spill it while it's hot

Journeys

Going far away

Passing a million stories

Just to write my own

Expectations

Believe I'm worthless

So that I might surprise you

And not let you down

Discord

Last online 2 weeks

please tell me it's all a joke

Unread forever

Anxiety

No one can hurt me

A thousand knives in my back

But I put them there

Unrequited

It's cold in my mind

Your smile keeps me unfrozen

But you'll never know

Lonely

It is dark in here

Shadows cluster in my mind

Choking out my joy

Escape

One day I'll be there

Where dreams and life can combine

I hope I make it

Flowers

Beautiful petals

They Cannot survive without

Dirty roots beneath

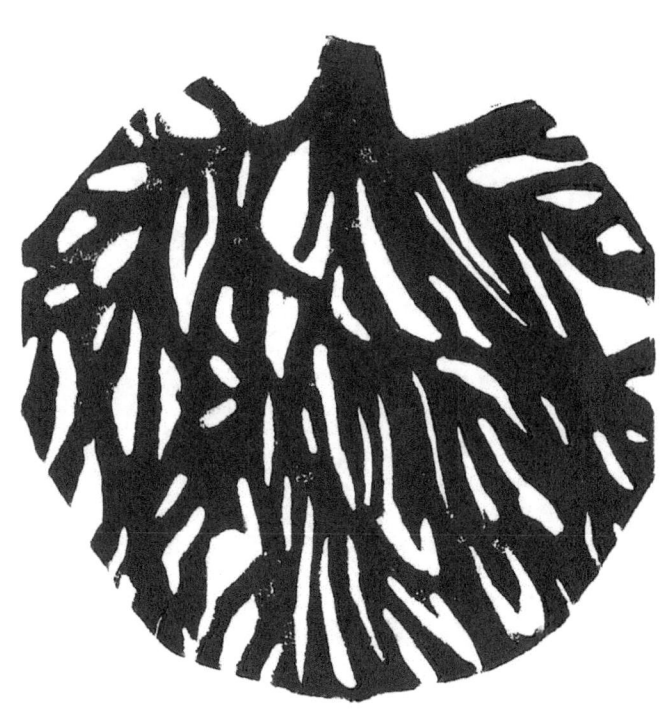

Dejected poetry

I'm Never finished

putting together strange words

but what is the point

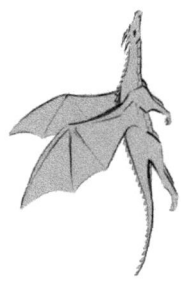

Explanation/Apology

I wrote all of these

some were forever ago

but now they are here

Ouch

AAA aaaa AAA aaa Aaaa

AAA AAAA aaa aaa aaa AAA AAA

AAAAAAAAAAAAAAAAAAAAA
AAAAAAAAAAAA
AAAAAAAAAAAAAh AaaAAAAA
AAAAAAAAAA

Birthday

A new year for you

To be whatever you want,

Be Someone you love

Escapist Dreams

An escape from life

Where anything can happen

Even happiness

Bees

Working every day

Keeping family alive

at risk to themselves

Anxiety

Bounded by a box

Fearing to reach beyond it,

Not real, strong as steel

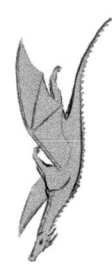

Depression

I envy atlas

Who only holds up the world

And not my demons

Sugar

A gold grown in earth

Brought from worker's broken backs

We are all addicts

poetry

Just words on a screen

but to some of us they are

Bottled emotions

The trouble of haiku

Try writing haiku

For someone who's astounding

I run out of space

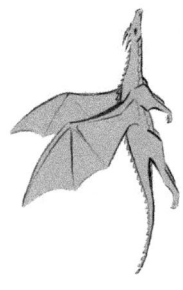

Grandma

Most beautiful gal

Sleeping here so peacefully

As machines flatline

Family reunion

Atop a green hill

We wear our best. I'm ready,

With flowers for graves

ASDF

Why did I write these

Look at these messes of words

hope I don't offend

Stabbing people

Please do not do it

Like seriously that hurts

and makes such a mess

Sick day

My mind is muted

Speaking dull thoughts stings my throat

And yet I'm still here

Mark B.

chats at 3 AM

Hey Man, I Love you, goodnight

My final goodbye

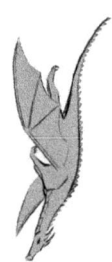

Cheese

true gold made from time

very classy and cultured

a goal to achieve

Sharing

Putting up poems

started panicking because

My soul's on display

human

watch us run, fall, cry

to live and die, try and fail

it's all we can do

Missing Reflection

Radiating light

Can't return the sentiment

My mirror's shattered

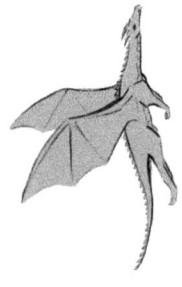

Coward's conversation

Hiding with light words

For stronger ones might destroy

Instead it's unsaid

Discordant Self

You should be happy

Everything is going well

Something must be wrong

time

there's never enough

too quick in good company

too slow when alone

Splat

The sunlight goes dim

The man looks up, something falls

Refrigerator

Fears

insufficiency

heights and failure, but mostly

being forgotten

Constellations

People give meaning

To tiny dots in the sky

Their shine doesn't change

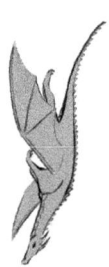

Silly Reasoning

Just a bunch of words

That never meant anything

How'd they make you feel

Early morning haiku

Words will fill my head

Of all the things I can Write

I just want to sleep

Angst

Angst aNgst anGst angSt angsT

AnGsT aNgSt AngSt AngsT ANgSt
Angst ANGST

anGst angST ANgst ANGST angsT

Insecurity

Sometimes I just need

Soft words and a reminder

That you don't hate me

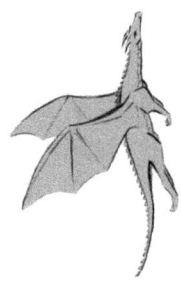

Perspective

Sometimes a dark room

Is what's required to see

The pinpricks of light

Impostor

What or where I am

I just cannot tell sometimes

Prove that I am real

Drowning

I can't ask for help

Even when it's so simple

I'd be a bother

Everything's fine

really I'm okay

like sure I might appear sad

but eh it's all fine

Socializing

Should have a good time

Surrounded by those I know

instead I'm alone

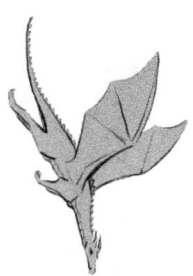

Dreams

Glorious what if's

Where marvelous things happen

ending each morning

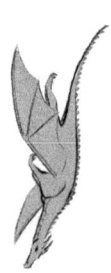

what if–

it's a disaster?

everything just falls apart?

the ending's happy?

learning

I am not the one

who has every true answer

but I can learn them

Hahaha haha ha

The joke falls in place

Realizing the punchline

Was me all along

Attention deficit

assignment deadlines

instead of working on them

I'm writing haiku

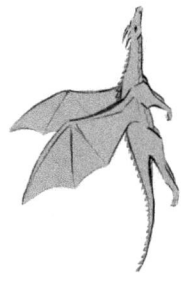

words

with repetition

something that once had value

becomes meaningless

My Friends

talented at art

sharing gorgeous creations

souls full of magic

Unbounding

Is there meaning here

That could take root in the soul

And escape shackles?

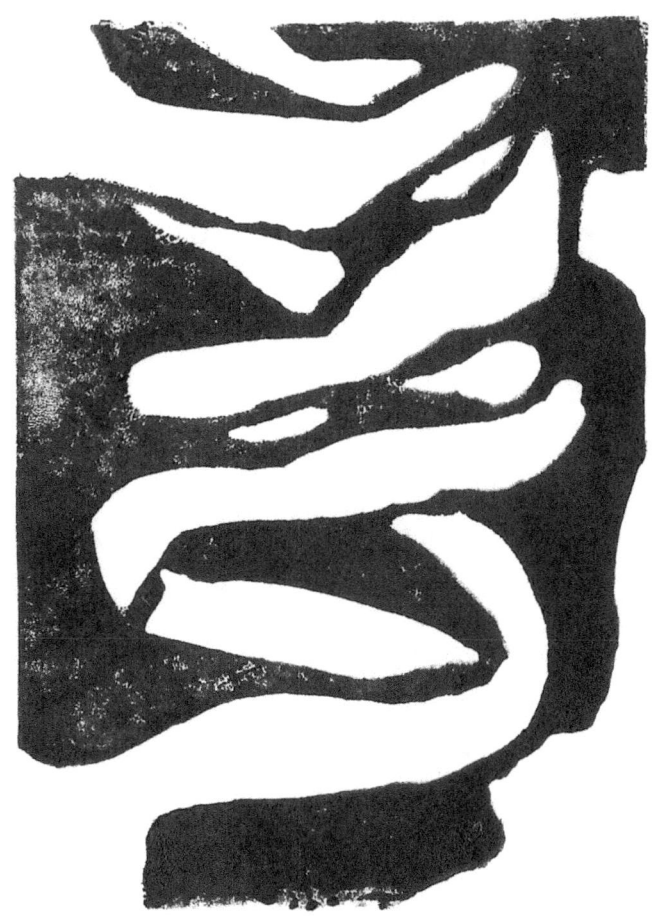

sharing words

written with intent

to express nascent feelings

how are they received?

Antecedent Duplication

If billions have lived

then everything I've written

is already done

Motivation

I just want to be

Remembered for something great

And not lost to time

Simple comfort

The world is so big

And I feel so small and frail

Except in your arms

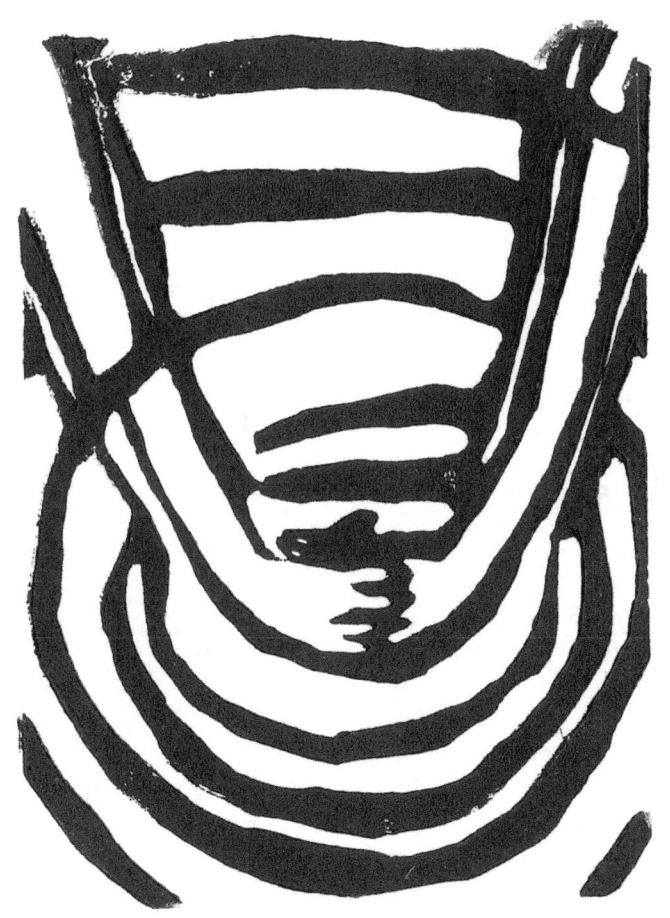

commonly unique

every grain of sand

with its own novel story

replaced every wave

unabashedly unoriginal

everything was said

long before our chance to speak

and yet we'll still talk

Craftsmanship

When no one knows who

Everything we make is ours

And they can't take it

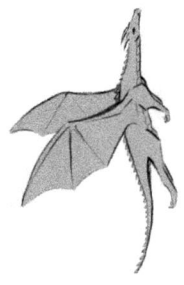

In touch

It has been a while

Since we last spoke together

I'll be a ghost too

Goner

If I fade away

Promise you won't forget me

Like everyone else

Anyone out there

Someone else should write

Something in here so it's not

Me monologuing

Writing these

Anyone can write

This short form of poetry

So give it a try

Scheming minds

We had many plans

But we couldn't save the world

Our plots, six feet deep

Friends pt 2

Specifically

Consideration advised

For your grand wonder

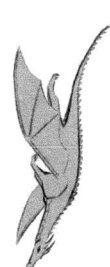

Knock knock

Okay, Well who's there

No one. I'm bad at punchlines

Ah well I should go

Jaded

Just a nice person

Without anything to hide

Except for old scars

Cowardice

I am a coward

One day I'll be different

In a nice wood box

Specialized Shyness

I could speak for hours

On things without real meaning,

not what's on my mind

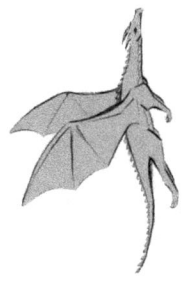

Burning out

Always thinking that

You can go another week

But it weighs you down

Hi

I am a haiku

collection of syllables

Just a pile of words

Uninstall

Stop all the worry

Go join the faceless masses

be lost forever

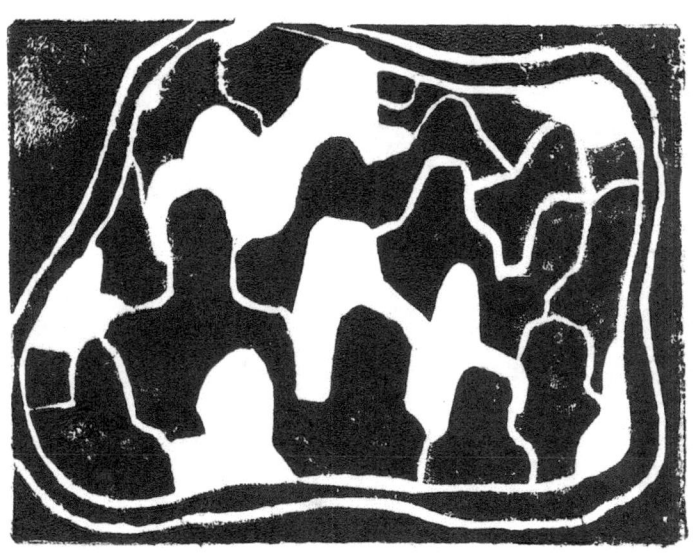

Otherwise

After reaching out

Everything could fall apart

Or it could improve

Friday

It's Friday my dudes

Anything fun happening?

Have a good weekend

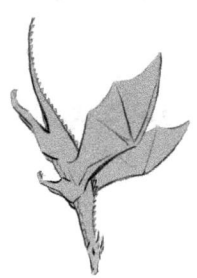

Surrender

I'm letting it win

In order to stop this war

I'll just stop feeling

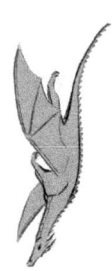

Missing

What is the purpose?

As there can't be an ending,

If it never starts

Simply Exasperated

haiku from a bath

So full of edgy nonsense

It has no meaning

Bad advice

If no one is told

Then you just have to survive

And they'll never know

Hidden costs

beware accepting

deals that you cannot afford

some costs are hidden

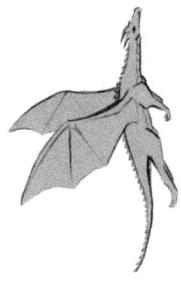

Out of stock

I'm all out of care

I spent it far too quickly

And I can't restock

a Smile

the simplest gesture

capable of showing and

hiding everything

One of those mornings

I don't want to be

And I don't even know why

Lost in the bad vibes

Busy

you cannot stop life

instead outmaneuver it

Don't let it beat you

Whatever this is

It attacks in waves

Making me forget reasons

To not hide away

Departing words

A short eulogy

For something never to be-

It could have been great

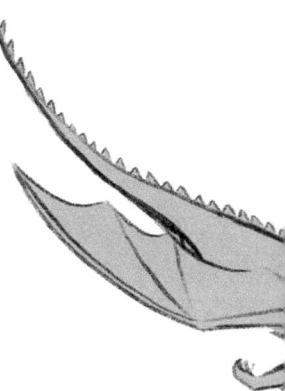